I   e

Kirklees COUNCIL

Culture & Leisure Services
Red Doles Lane
Huddersfield, West Yorks HD2 1YF

**This book should be returned on or before the latest date
stamped below. *Fines are charged if the item is late.***

DEWSBURY LIBRARY
01924 - 3?5080   "/14

KT-470-799

Katie Dicker and Sam Sheldon

WAYLAND

800 484 401

KIRKLEES LIBRARIES

Published in paperback in 2014 by Wayland

Copyright © Wayland 2014

Wayland
Hachette Children's Books
338 Euston Road
London NW1 3BH

Wayland Australia
Level 17/207 Kent Street
Sydney, NSW 2000

All rights reserved. Apart from any use permitted
under UK copyright law, this publication may only be
reproduced, stored or transmitted, in any form, or by
any means with prior permission in writing of the
publishers or in the case of reprographic production in
accordance with the terms of licences issued by the
Copyright Licensing Agency.

Managing Editor: Rasha Elsaeed

Produced for Wayland by
White-Thomson Publishing Ltd.
www.wtpub.co.uk
+44 (0)843 208 7460

Editor: Katie Dicker
Designer: Clare Nicholas
Editorial consultant: Daniel Owers
Photographer: Chris Fairclough

All rights reserved.

British Library Cataloguing in Publication Data
Dicker, Katie
  I belong to the Jewish faith
  1. Judaism - Juvenile literature
  I. Title II. Sheldon, Sam
  296

ISBN 978 0 7502 8428 8

Printed in China

Wayland is a division of Hachette Children's Books,
an Hachette UK company.
www.hachette.co.uk

Acknowledgements
The author and publisher would like to thank the
following people for their help and participation in
this book:
The Sheldon family, Victoria Flint,
Deborah Rozansky, Rabbi Rodney Mariner
and all at Belsize Square Synagogue.

The website addresses (URLs) included in this book
were valid at the time of going to press. However,
because of the nature of the Internet, it is possible
that some addresses may have changed, or sites may
have changed or closed down since publication. While
the author and publisher regret any inconvenience
this may cause the readers, no responsibility for any
such changes can be accepted by either the author
or the publisher.

Disclaimer
The text in this book is based on the experience of
one family. While every effort has been made to offer
accurate and clearly expressed information, the author
and publisher acknowledge that some explanations
may not be relevant to those who practise their faith
in a different way.

10 9 8 7 6 5 4 3 2 1

Contents

The Sabbath

Hi, I'm Sam. It's Friday night and it's the start of the **Sabbath**. My family are Jewish. We're about to have dinner together. Before we eat, we wash our hands and we say a **prayer**.

Mum lights the candles just before sunset on Friday to show that the Sabbath has begun.

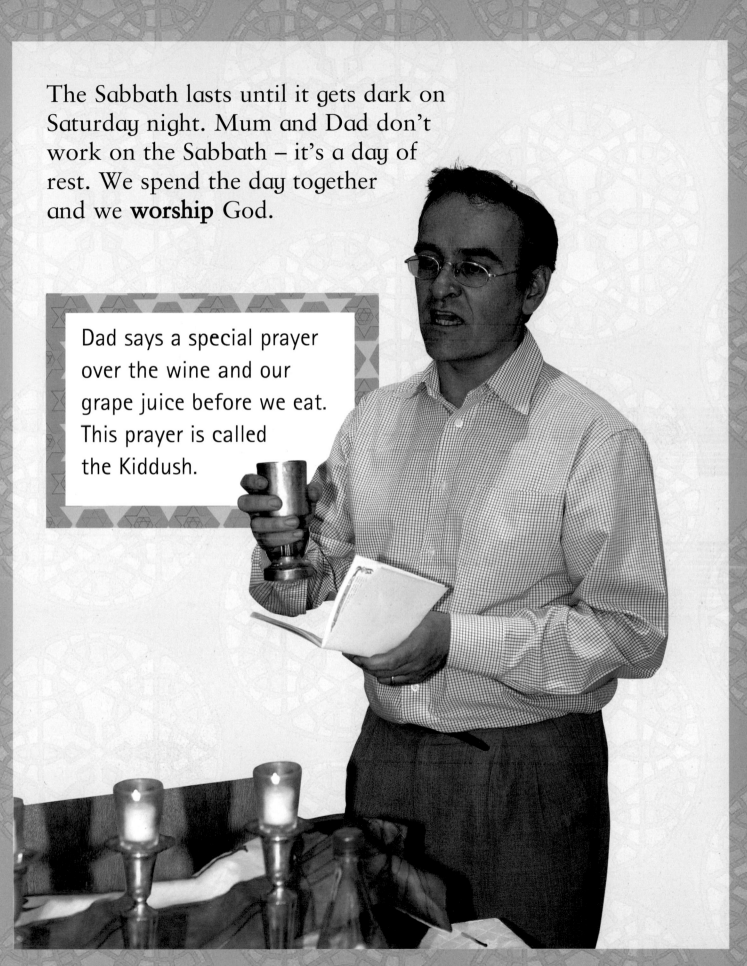

The Sabbath lasts until it gets dark on Saturday night. Mum and Dad don't work on the Sabbath – it's a day of rest. We spend the day together and we **worship** God.

Dad says a special prayer over the wine and our grape juice before we eat. This prayer is called the Kiddush.

Talking to God

We use a prayer book, called the Siddur, to talk to God. When we pray, we thank God for what he has given us. We ask God to help us and to help other people, too.

On Saturday night, we say prayers around the **Havdalah candle**, a box of spices and a full cup of wine to welcome the week ahead.

I wear a cotton cap called a kippah to show my respect for God. God created the world and he looks after us. I try to do as God would wish every day.

Every time I come home, I touch this wooden box by the front door. It's called a **mezuzah** and reminds me this is a Jewish home.

At the synagogue

We go to the **synagogue** on Saturday morning to worship God. The service is lead by the **Rabbi**. He reads stories from the **Torah** to us, about God's power.

The Rabbi holds up the Torah so we can all see what has been read. We listen to a different story every week.

The Torah scrolls are stored in a special cupboard called the Ark. They contain the five books of Moses, from the **Bible**. They are kept in velvet cases decorated with silver.

This is the Cantor standing in front of the Ark. During the service, the Cantor invites us to sing the prayers with him.

Learning about Judaism

We learn a lot about **Judaism** from the Rabbi. He is very wise. He gives a talk during the service at the synagogue. He teaches us to be kind to others and to help people in need.

I'm not old enough to read the Torah yet, but the Rabbi explains to me what the words of Hebrew mean.

There are Hebrew classes at the synagogue, and I go there to learn more about Judaism, too. We read Bible stories and we learn about the history of the Jewish people.

The Rabbi is showing me a Torah scroll decoration. He is very good at explaining all the Jewish traditions.

The Torah

The Torah is written in Hebrew. This is the language that Jews speak in Israel. It takes about a year for the **scribes** to write the Torah by hand.

We're not allowed to touch the Torah, but we use a pointer called a yad to follow God's words.

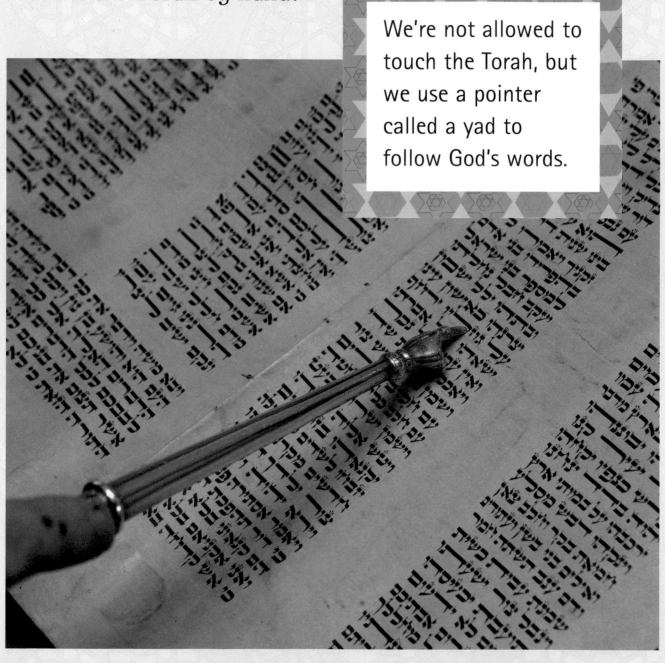

A different part of the Torah is read each week. It takes a year to finish it. When the whole Torah has been read we celebrate **Simchat Torah.**

At Simchat Torah, men carry the Torah scrolls around the synagogue seven times. We sing to praise God as we follow them.

Abraham and Moses

Abraham was the first Jew. He was chosen by God to teach people to worship just one God – our creator. We are all **descendants** of Abraham and think about his teachings in our lives, too.

Lily and I read Bible stories about Abraham. He lived in Israel about 3,000 years ago.

Moses led the Jewish people from slavery in Egypt, to freedom. God gave Moses the **Ten Commandments** at Mount Sinai. These laws are written in the Torah.

Mum teaches at the synagogue. Today, she's telling us how brave the Jews were when they escaped from Egypt.

15

Sukkot

In the autumn, we celebrate **Sukkot**. We make a shelter called a Sukkah. We put up a tent in the garden and we decorate it with fruit, leaves, branches and pictures.

During Sukkot, we eat all our meals in the Sukkah. It's good fun! Sukkot lasts for a week.

The Sukkah reminds us of the Jews' escape from Egypt. They had to sleep in tents in the desert. Sukkot is also a harvest festival when we thank God for giving us the food we eat.

We make a Sukkah at the synagogue, too, for everyone to see. Lily and I are hanging these fruit to decorate it.

17

Special food

The Torah says we're not allowed to eat some foods, such as pork and shellfish. All our food has to be prepared in a special way. We call the foods we can eat 'kosher'.

I'm saying a prayer over these two loaves. They remind us that God provided extra food for the Jews in the desert on Fridays, before **Shabbat**.

At **Passover**, we celebrate the Jews' escape from Egypt. We have a big meal called a seder that reminds us we are no longer slaves. We serve our food on a seder plate.

We fill the seder plate with different food. The **matzah**, for example, reminds us that the Jews escaped in a hurry before the bread could rise.

Jewish festivals

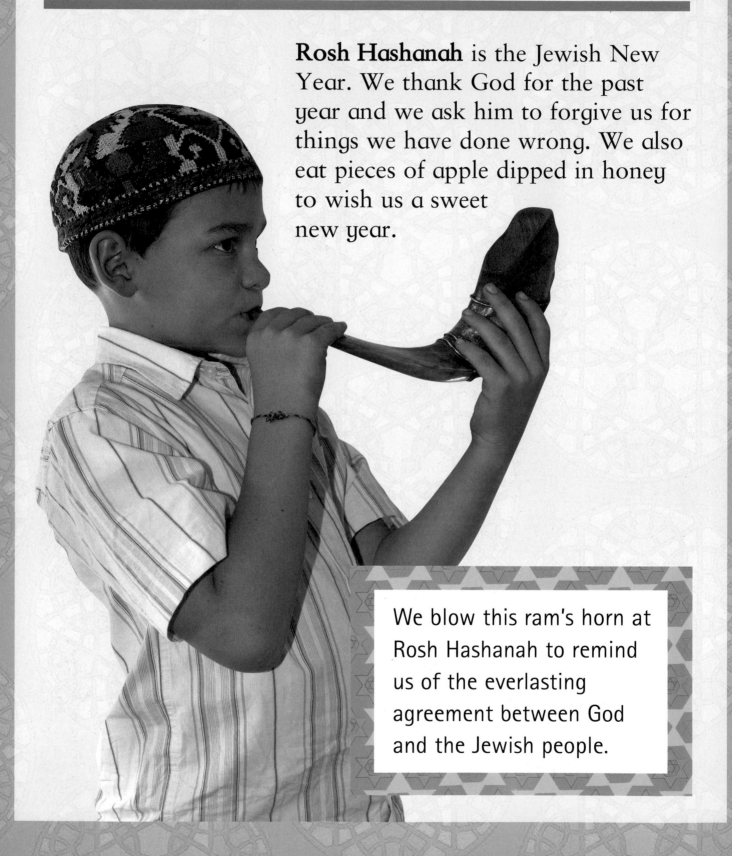

Rosh Hashanah is the Jewish New Year. We thank God for the past year and we ask him to forgive us for things we have done wrong. We also eat pieces of apple dipped in honey to wish us a sweet new year.

We blow this ram's horn at Rosh Hashanah to remind us of the everlasting agreement between God and the Jewish people.

At **Hanukkah**, we celebrate the day the Jews regained their holy temple in Jerusalem. We play games and we give presents to each other. We also eat doughnuts and potato pancakes called latkes.

During Hanukkah, we light a candle on the hanukia each day. It reminds us that the oil found in the holy temple lasted for eight days.

Glossary and further information

Bible – a special book which tells the story of God's relationship with the Jewish people.

descendants – people who belong to the same family over many generations.

Havdalah candle – a braided, multi-wicked candle.

Judaism – the Jewish religion.

matzah – flat bread made from flour and water (but no yeast to make it rise).

mezuzah – a wooden box containing a piece of paper with a prayer from the Torah on it.

prayer – a way of talking to God.

Rabbi – a special Jewish teacher who is usually also the spiritual leader of the community.

Sabbath – the Jewish holy day. Also called **Shabbat** in Hebrew.

scribe – a person who writes a scroll.

synagogue – a building where Jews go to worship God.

Ten Commandments – ten rules given by God about how to behave.

Torah – a book full of God's words.

worship – to show love and respect to God.

Did you know?

- There are about 12 million Jews today, mostly living in Israel and the United States.
- There are different types of Jews. Jews can be called Orthodox, Reform, Conservative or Liberal.
- The dates of Jewish festivals follow a lunar calendar.

Activities

1. Arrange to visit a local synagogue. Write down the things you can see. What is the building used for?
2. How many Jewish festivals can you name? Find the name of a festival you have not heard of before. What is it about?
3. Read a story about the Jews from the first five books of the Bible. Draw a picture about this story.

Books to read

- *What Makes Someone a Jew?* by Lauren Seidman, Jewish Lights Publishing, 2007
- *Jewish Stories (Storyteller)* by Anita Ganeri, Evans Brothers, 2006

Websites

http://atschool.eduweb.co.uk/carolrb/judaism/judai1.html
A basic introduction to Judaism for primary school children, with clear text and colourful illustrations.

http://www.hitchams.suffolk.sch.uk/synagogue/index.htm
This website introduces children to life at a synagogue and daily life as a Jew, with simple text and colour photographs.

Organisations

The Board of Deputies of British Jews
6 Bloomsbury Square
London
WC1A 2LP

Jewish festivals

Rosh Hashanah (Sept / Oct)
The Jewish New Year.

Yom Kippur (Sept / Oct)
The holiest day in the Jewish calendar. Jews fast for 25 hours and spend the day in prayer.

Tabernacles (Sukkot) (Sept / Oct)
A harvest festival to remember the Jews' escape from Egypt through the desert.

Simchat Torah (October)
A festival to celebrate the end of the year's reading of the Torah.

Hanukkah (December)
A festival of lights, to remember the Jews' return to their temple in Jerusalem.

Pesach (Passover) (March / April)
A festival celebrating the time that Moses helped the Jews escape from Egypt.

Jewish symbols

Star of David – a symbol of the Jews. David was a Jewish King. The star is made from two triangles that overlap. Some people think this shows that Jews are inseparable and live a balanced life.

Menorah – a candelabrum with seven candle holders. The menorah was first used to decorate the tabernacle (moving temple) when the Jews travelled in the desert.

Index